Sassy Sally and Her Little Dog Suzi Celebrate Birthdays

(The Early Stages Series)

by Amber Stewart

There once lived a little girl named Sally.
God made Sally different than other kids.
Sally couldn't move, so God gave her a fancy chair.
Her chair had wheels and was her favorite color: pink.
Sally had a special job in life; to share hope with others.

Sally used a special machine called a ventilator to help her breathe because her muscles were too weak for her to breathe on her own. Her nurse, Sammy, would strap the machine to Sally's wheelchair, and she would zoom around in her chair with her little dog, Suzi.

Suzi and Sally were best friends.
Suzi made Sally very happy and helped her get through hard days with a smile on her face.

Sally and her little dog Suzi had birthdays close together, so they decided they would celebrate each other!

Sally invited all the dogs in the neighborhood,
and Suzi delivered invitations to all the people who were special to Sally.

Suzi even helped Sally decorate; but tying balloons with paws isn't easy, so Nurse Sammy lent them a hand.
They both wore beautiful dresses and Suzi even let Sally
put a big sparkly bow in her hair.

Sally was secretly nervous that people wouldn't come to the party. Sometimes it was hard for her to make new friends because she was different. Either way, she hoped that Suzi would feel special and loved. Nurse Sammy even helped Sally give Suzi a bath just for the occasion.

Both girls made special cakes for each other (with Sammy's help, of course!) and welcomed their friends. To Sally's surprise, everyone came and happily celebrated her! Suzi was happy to see her playmates came too, bearing bones with her name on them.

The guests brought lots of gifts and fun was had by all.
They watched a movie and played games.
Tug-of-war was both of their favorites!
Suzi chomped down on one end,
while Sally tied the other end to her chair.
What fun!

After the party guests had all gone home, Suzi jumped up in Sally's lap and they took off on a stroll around the block while reminiscing about the wonderful day they both had.

Sally gave Suzi a special treat she made for her,
and Suzi kissed her whole face as a way of saying thanks.

"Why are birthdays so special, anyway, Sally?" asked Suzi.
"Birthdays are special because life is a precious gift. Some live a long time. Others, not so much… but every life matters and everyone has a purpose. Do you know what that purpose is, Suzi?"

"To hide as many treats as possible?" asked Suzi.
"No, silly!" replied Sally.
"Our purpose is to love. Love each other and everyone else,
and show others that Jesus loves them the most."
"Does Jesus love everyone? Even little dogs like me?" asked Suzi.
"Jesus loves you and me and every creature,
down to the tiniest bumblebee," said Sally.

"Jesus loves you so much that He made you just for me!" Sally continued. "If we admit that we're not perfect and ask Jesus to come into our hearts, He will put a beautiful light inside of us so the whole world can see Him through us."
"Wow! Like a lightening bug? Sign me up!" said Suzi.

"Like a glow stick!" said Sally, "but glow sticks have to be broken before they can shine the brightest. People are like that, too. People glow through what they go through. That's why birthdays are special, Suzi. God has blessed us with another year together to share His love with others. That's enough reason to celebrate!" said Sally.

Suzi knew that Sally was born very sick, and the doctor said she wouldn't have a long life, but she proved everyone wrong and was growing up with Suzi. Suzi was thankful to have a best friend in Sally, and Sally felt the same way about her sweet little Suzi.

"I love you, Sally," said Suzi.

"I love you, Suzi. I love Jesus, too. And we love because He first loved us."

"Amen to that!" said Suzi.

"If you know Jesus and Jesus knows you, He will help you get through the hard times in life and give you JOY!" said Sally.
"Happiness comes and goes,
but joy only comes when Jesus lives in your heart and lasts forever!
Joy puts peace in your heart and a smile on your face."
"The world would be a better place if more people had joy," replied Suzi.

Just then, the ice cream truck pulled up! What perfect timing!
"Want a pup cup?" asked Sally.
"You know it! And your favorite vanilla and chocolate twist?"
"The best of both worlds!" cheered Sally.
"God must really love us!" exclaimed Suzi.
"More than we'll ever know" replied Sally.
What a great birthday!

Printed in the USA
CPSIA information can be obtained
at www.ICGtesting.com
LVHW060043010224
770422LV00014B/122